ADVENTURE TIME™

TOTALLY RAD BOOK OF SECRETS

PSS!
PRICE STERN SLOAN
An Imprint of Penguin Group (USA) LLC

PRICE STERN SLOAN
Published by the Penguin Group
Penguin Group (USA) LLC, 375 Hudson Street, New York, New York 10014, USA

USA | Canada | UK | Ireland | Australia | New Zealand | India | South Africa | China

penguin.com
A Penguin Random House Company

Published in 2014 by Price Stern Sloan, a division of Penguin Young Readers Group,
345 Hudson Street, New York, New York 10014. PSS! is a registered trademark of
Penguin Group (USA) LLC. Manufactured in China.

ISBN 978-0-8431-8011-4   10 9 8 7 6 5 4 3 2 1

Welcome, dream weavers, to your new *Totally Rad Book of Secrets!*

In this book, you can write whatever you want. Really, anything; we won't look. We are here to encourage you to write about your deepest fears (it's not like we'll use them against you) and biggest hopes (but we will definitely, definitely NOT laugh at them). So please, go ahead—fill these pages to your heart's content.

With love and secretitude,
Your *Adventure Time* Overlords

(Finn & Jake)

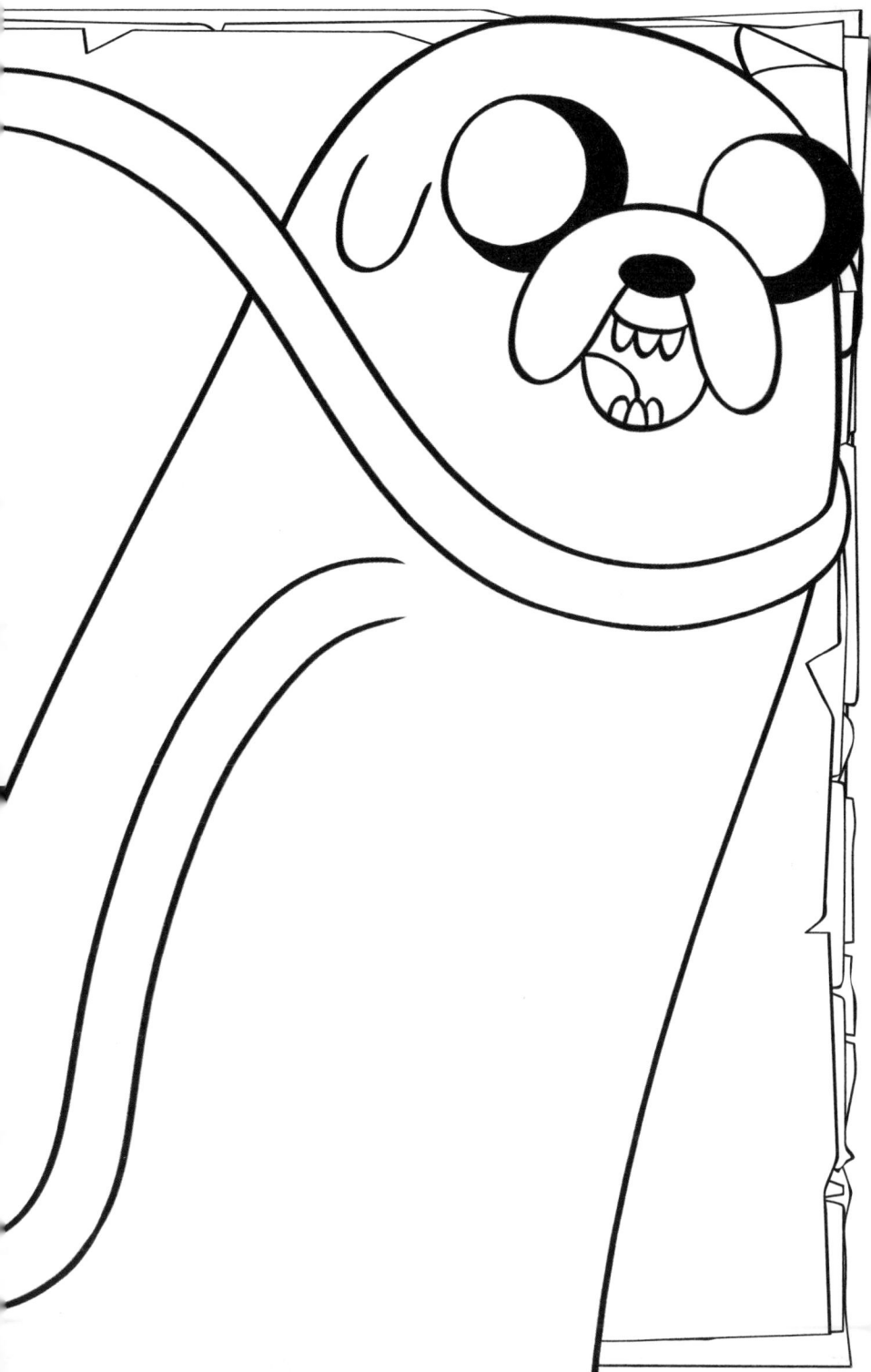

Hmmm, what awesome stuff should I do today? Jake suit? Strangle some pixies? High-five harder than anyone has ever high-fived before? Meh, I might just sit here and play tic-tac-toe by myself.

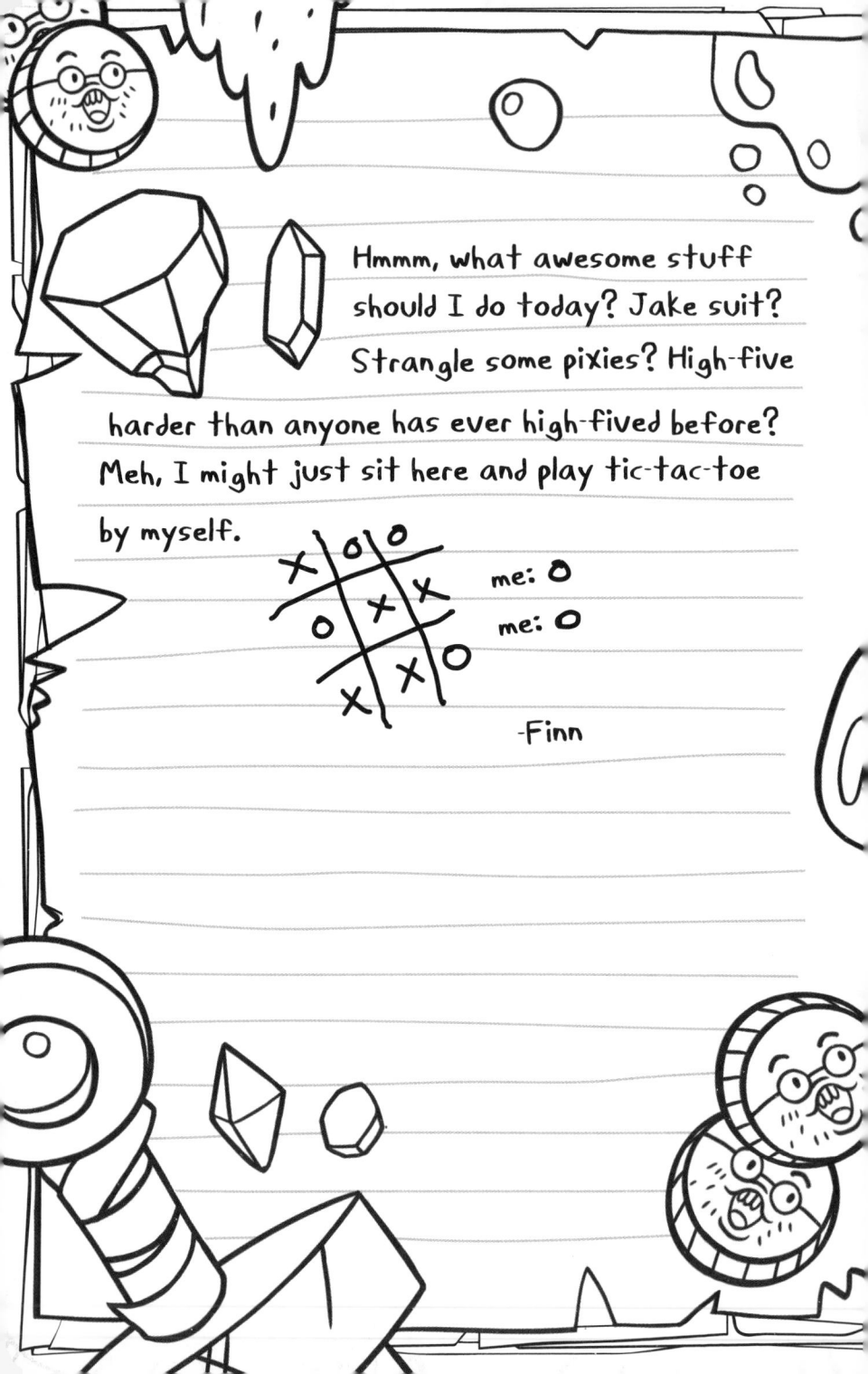

me: O

me: O

-Finn

Arrgh! Daddy totally ate my fries today.
Even after I told him not to — he ate them!
Why does he always do stuff like this to me?
I really wanted those fries! It's like he doesn't
even get me at all. I'm going to write a song
about it . . . that'll show him.

-Marceline

Oh my glob, all these guys are, like, totally all over my lumps, totally all the time. I look fresh to death today, and everyone was, like, seriously noticing my new dress and bag. This day is coming out awesome!

-LSP

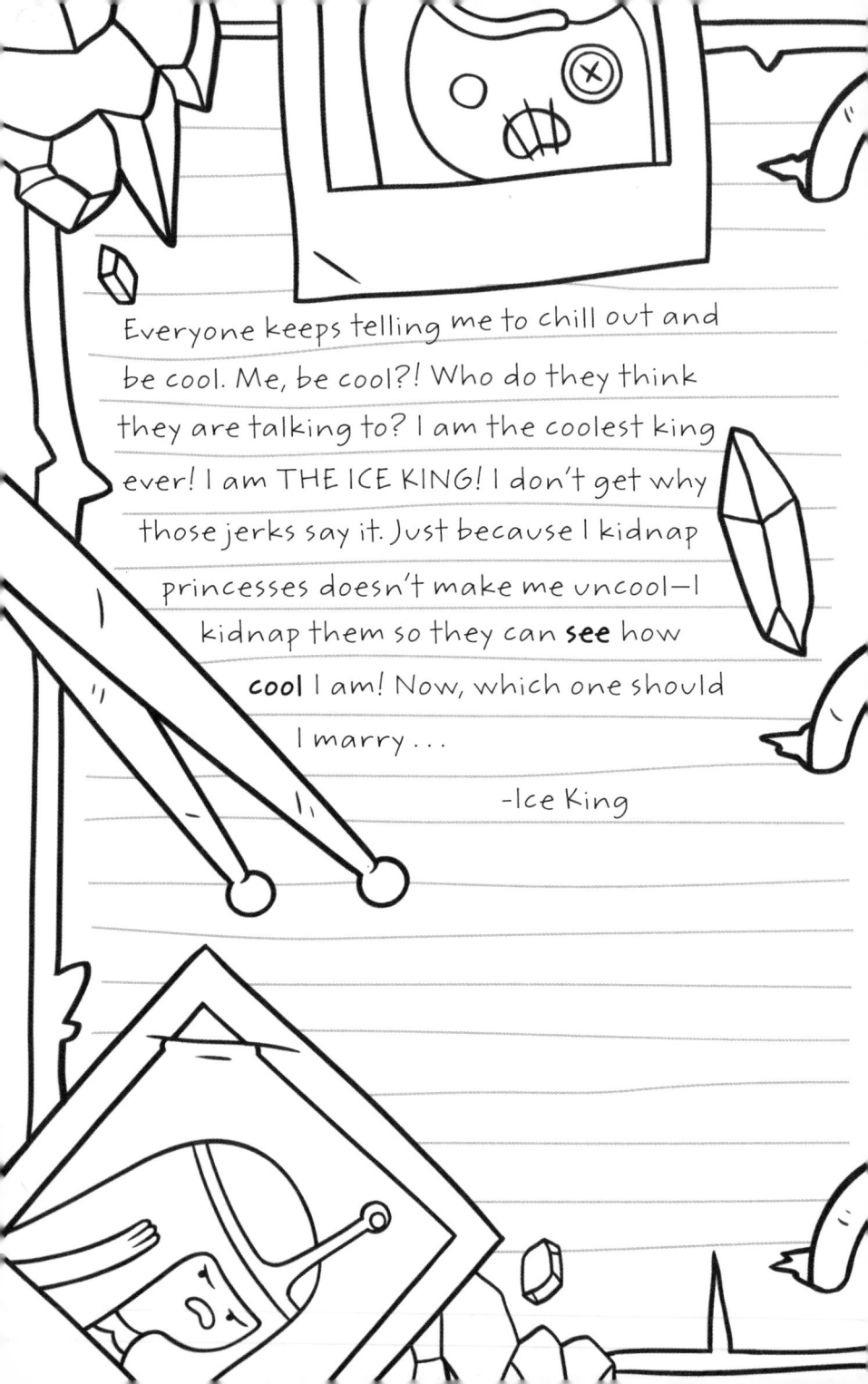

Everyone keeps telling me to chill out and be cool. Me, be cool?! Who do they think they are talking to? I am the coolest king ever! I am THE ICE KING! I don't get why those jerks say it. Just because I kidnap princesses doesn't make me uncool—I kidnap them so they can **see** how **cool** I am! Now, which one should I marry...

-Ice King

FOOTBALL, I KNOW YOU READ THIS WHEN I'M NOT HOME. GO AWAY. THIS IS NOT FOR YOU.

I'M DEADLY SERIOUS.

AND NOW MY SECRETS...

OOH, OOH, TODAY, FINN AND I PLAYED VIDEO GAMES! AND THEN, I BEAT JAKE AT A GAME WHERE WE WERE THROWING THINGS AT OTHER THINGS, AND NOW HE HAS TO CALL ME SENSEI FOR A

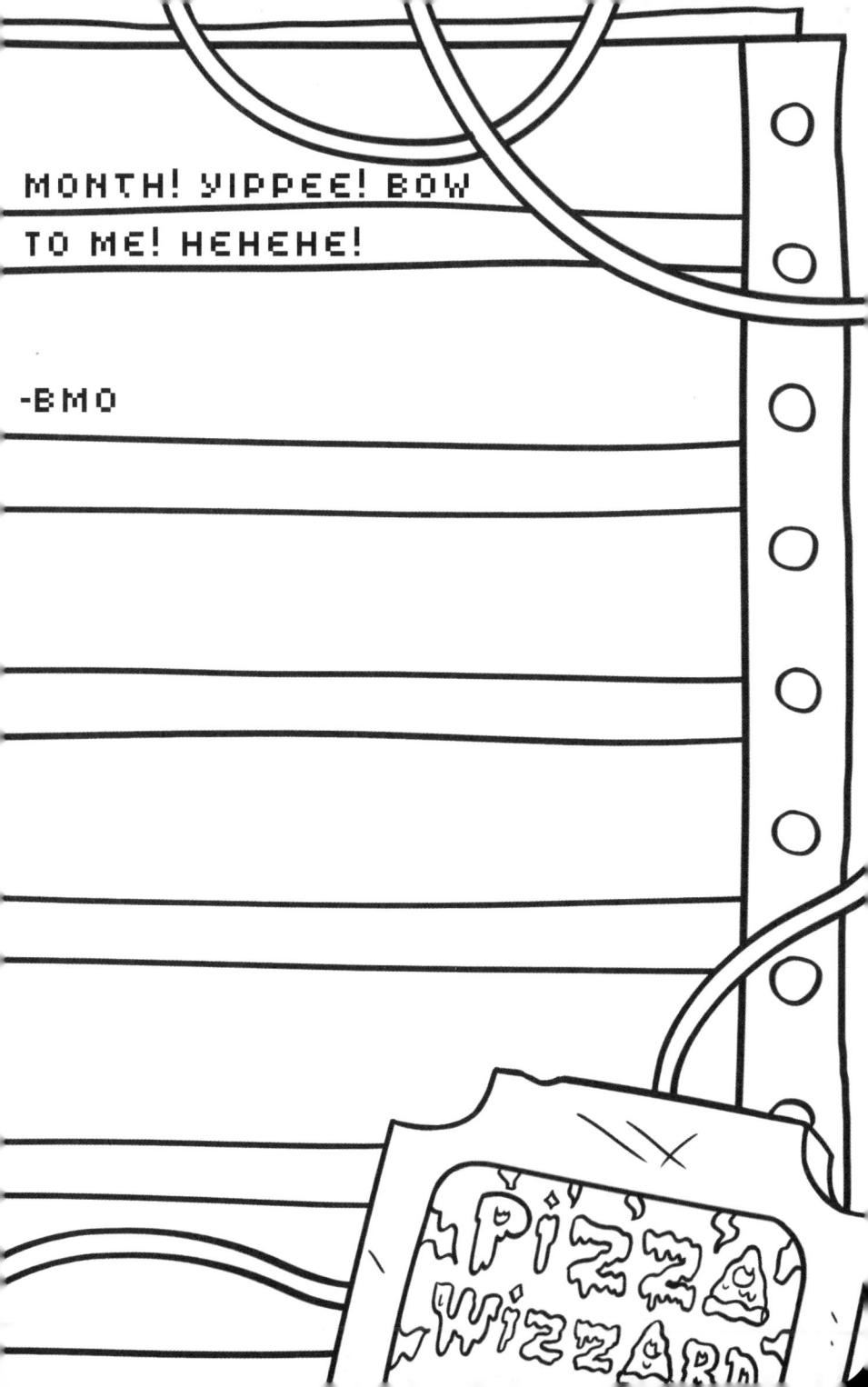

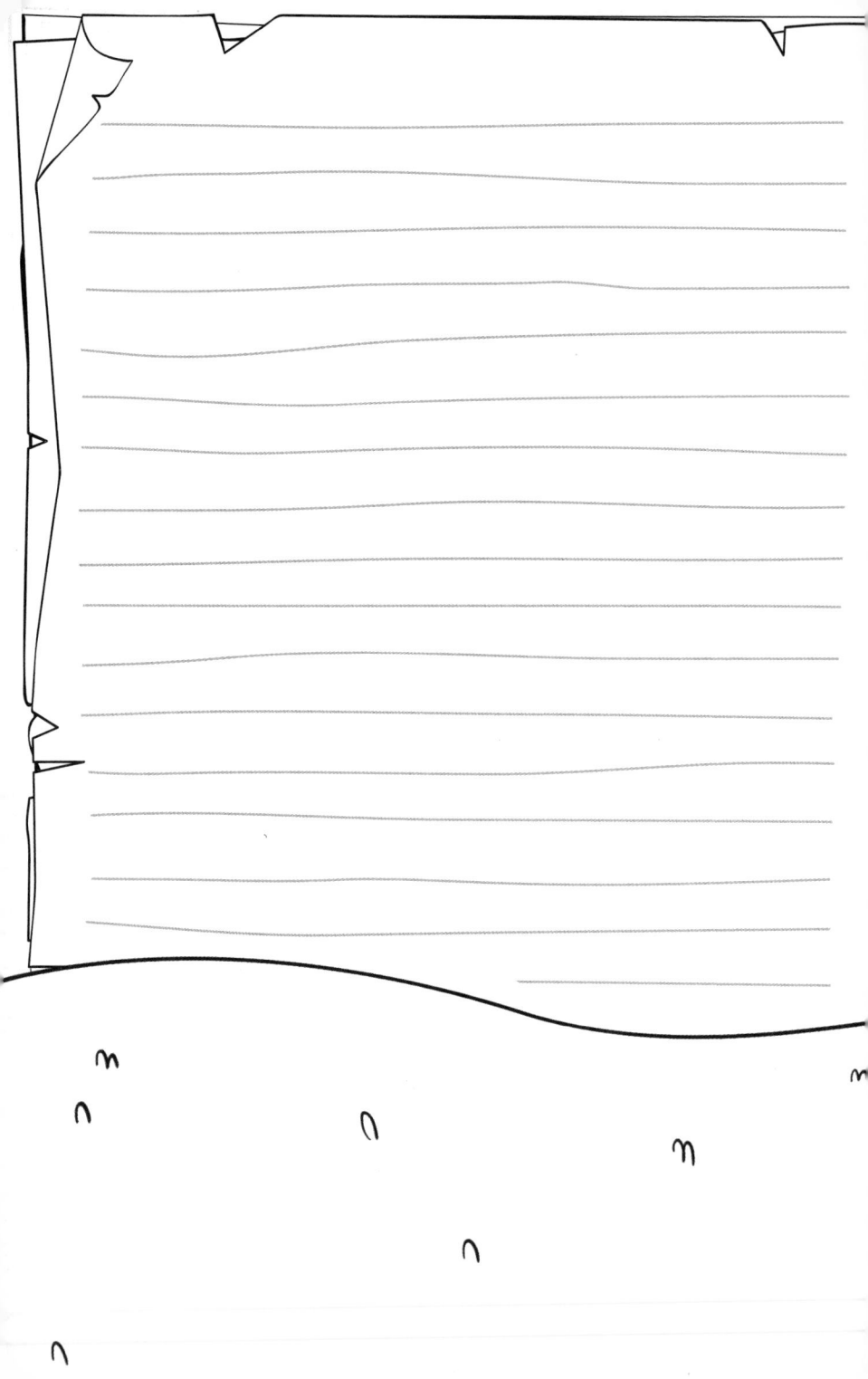

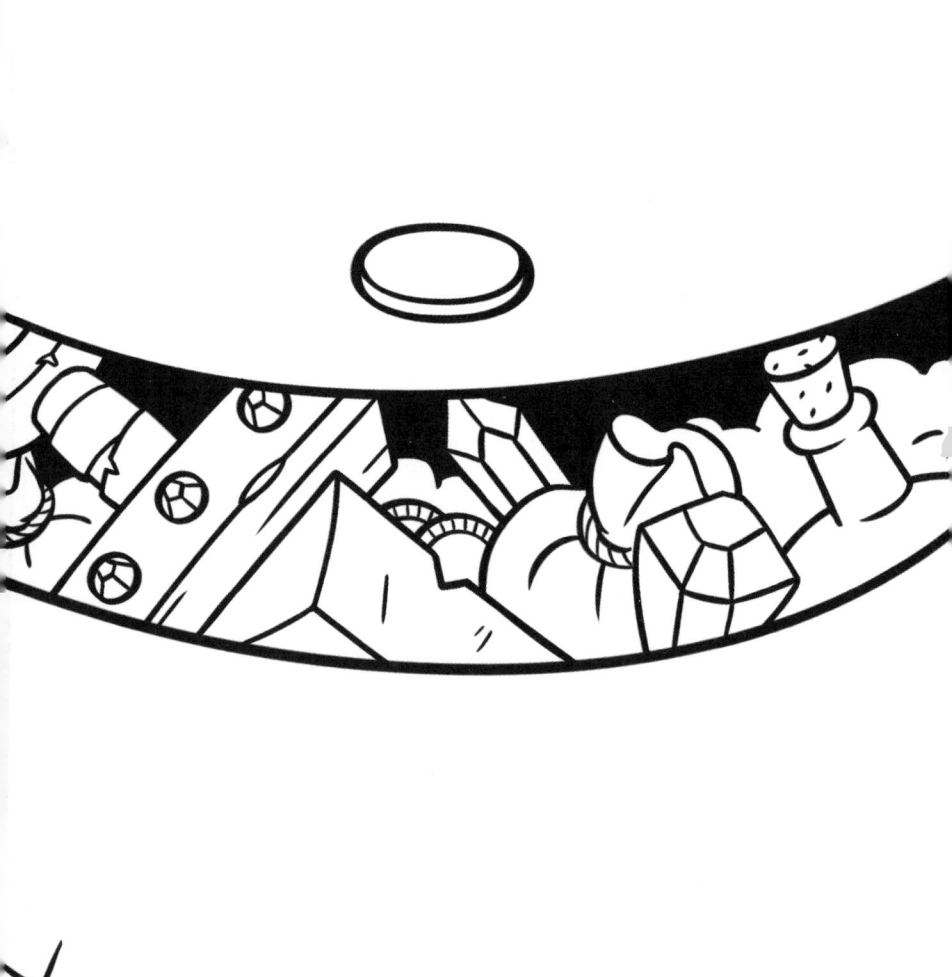